I0804459

The INSIDE GUIDE

EARLY AMERICAN HISTORY

The American Revolution

By Bert Wilberforce

Cavendish Square

Published in 2024 by Cavendish Square Publishing, LLC
2544 Clinton Street Buffalo, NY 14224

Website: cavendishsq.com

Disclaimer: Portions of this work were originally authored by Nicole Shea and published as *The American Revolution* (The Story of America). All new material this edition authored by Bert Wilberforce.

All websites were available and accurate when this book was sent to press.

Library of Congress Cataloging-in-Publication Data

Names: Wilberforce, Bert, author.
Title: The American Revolution / Bert Wilberforce.
Description: Buffalo, New York : Cavendish Square Publishing, [2024] |
Series: The inside guide: early American history | Includes index.
Identifiers: LCCN 2022053543 (print) | LCCN 2022053544 (ebook) | ISBN 9781502667670 (library binding) | ISBN 9781502667663 (paperback) | ISBN 9781502667687 (ebook)
Subjects: LCSH: United States–History–Revolution, 1775-1783–Causes–Juvenile literature.
Classification: LCC E210 .W55 2024 (print) | LCC E210 (ebook) | DDC 973.3/11–dc22
LC record available at https://lccn.loc.gov/2022053543
LC ebook record available at https://lccn.loc.gov/2022053544

Editor: Therese Shea
Designer: Deanna Paternostro

The photographs in this book are used by permission and through the courtesy of: Cover Everett Collection/Shutterstock.com; p. 4 Map of territorial growth 1775/Wikimedia Commons; p. 6 Proof sheet of one penny stamps Stamp Act 1765/Wikimedia Commons; p. 7 Parliament Stamp Act1765/Wikimedia Commons; p. 8 The Boston Massacre MET DT2086/Wikimedia Commons; p. 9 Boston Tea Party w/Wikimedia Commons; p. 10 Flickr - USCapitol - The First Continental Congress, 1774/Wikimedia Commons; pp. 11, 12 Courtesy of the Library of Congress; p. 13 jejim/Shutterstock.com; p. 15 Victorian Traditions/Shutterstock.com; p. 16 The Death of General Warren at the Battle of Bunker's Hill/Wikimedia Commons; p. 18 Bunker Hill by Pyle/Wikimedia Commons; p. 20 United States Declaration of Independence/Wikimedia Commons; p. 21 Washington Crossing the Delaware by Emanuel Leutze, MMA-NYC, 1851/Wikimedia Commons; p. 22 Surrender of General Burgoyne/Wikimedia Commons; p. 24 aimintang/iStock Photo; p. 25 Molly Pitcher currier ives/ Wikimedia Commons; p. 26 Battle of Guilford Courthouse 15 March 1781/Wikimedia Commons; p. 27 Surrender of Lord Cornwallis/ Wikimedia Commons; p. 29 (left) BattleofLongisland/Wikimedia Commons; p. 29 (right) Declaration of Independence (1819), by John Trumbull/Wikimedia Commons.

CPSIA compliance information: Batch #CSCSQ24: For further information contact Cavendish Square Publishing LLC at 1-877-980-4450.

Printed in the United States of America

CONTENTS

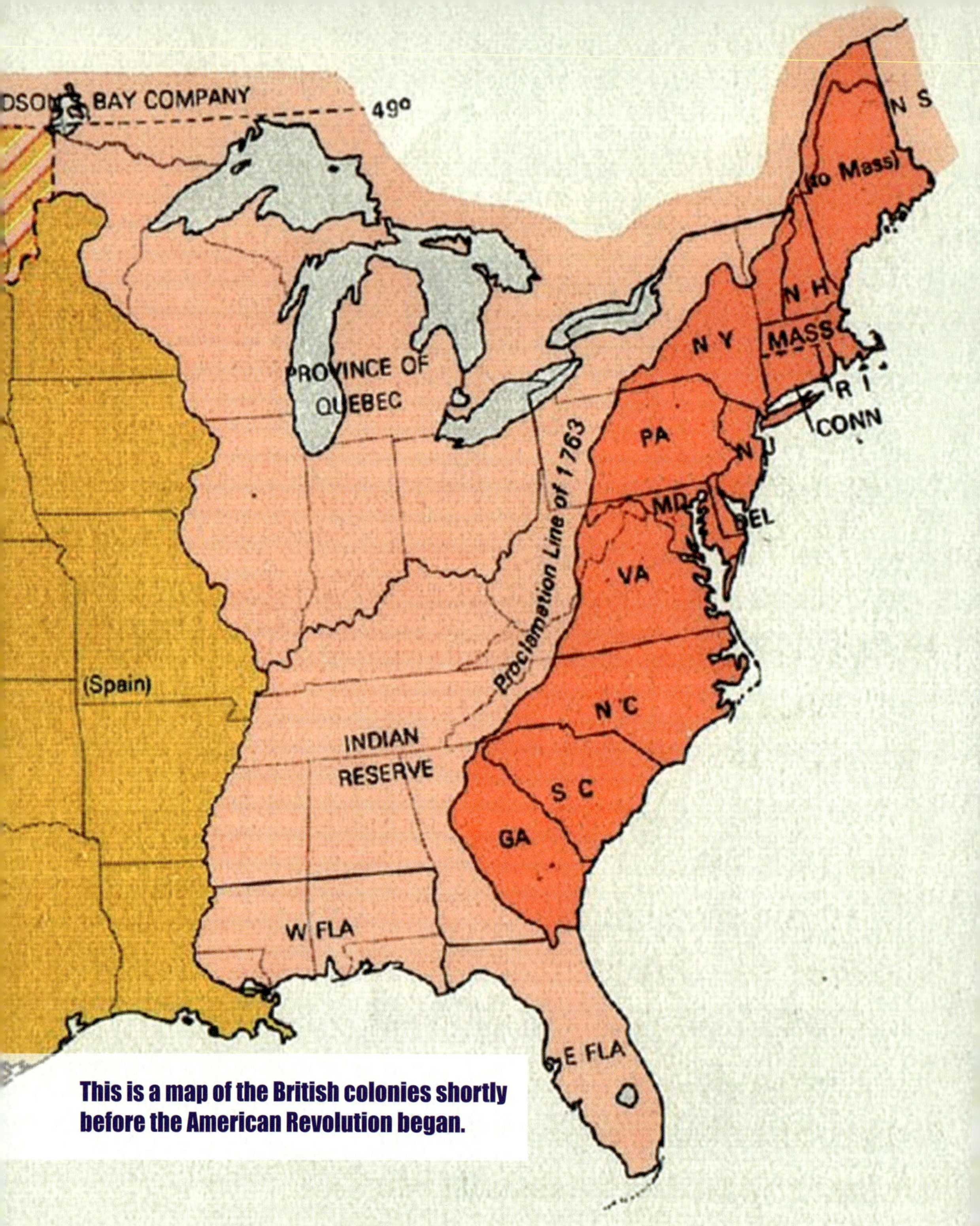

This is a map of the British colonies shortly before the American Revolution began.

THE SEEDS OF REVOLUTION

Chapter One

The outcome of the American Revolution seems unlikely when you think about it. There were just 2.5 million people in the British colonies at the time. About 8 million people lived in Great Britain, and the British Empire was vast and powerful. Many events occurred that paved the way for the colonists' victory. Years before the war began, British policies began to stir up frustration and anger in the colonies, causing some to argue that independence was necessary.

Unpopular Taxes

A poor British economy in the 1760s and 1770s contributed to the start of the revolution. Great Britain had spent a lot of money fighting wars and was in financial trouble. The British looked for ways to raise money. They soon looked to their colonies in North America.

The British government imposed taxes on its colonies under the Sugar Act of 1764. It placed a tax on other countries' sugar and molasses (and other items such as fabric), so the

Fast Fact

Founding Father John Adams said, "The Revolution was effected before the war **commenced**. The Revolution was in the minds and hearts of the people."

Fast Fact

Britain and France fought the Seven Years' War (1756–1763) in Europe, North America, and India. Conflicts between these nations in North America were called the French and Indian War.

colonists would be forced to buy British sugar, molasses, and other products. In 1765, the British issued the Stamp Act, taxing legal documents, newspapers, and even playing cards in the colonies. That same year, Britain issued the Quartering Act, which required colonists to house (quarter) and feed British troops.

Without representatives in the British **Parliament**, colonists had no say in these laws and taxes. When Britain introduced the Townshend Acts in 1767—taxing paint, paper, lead,

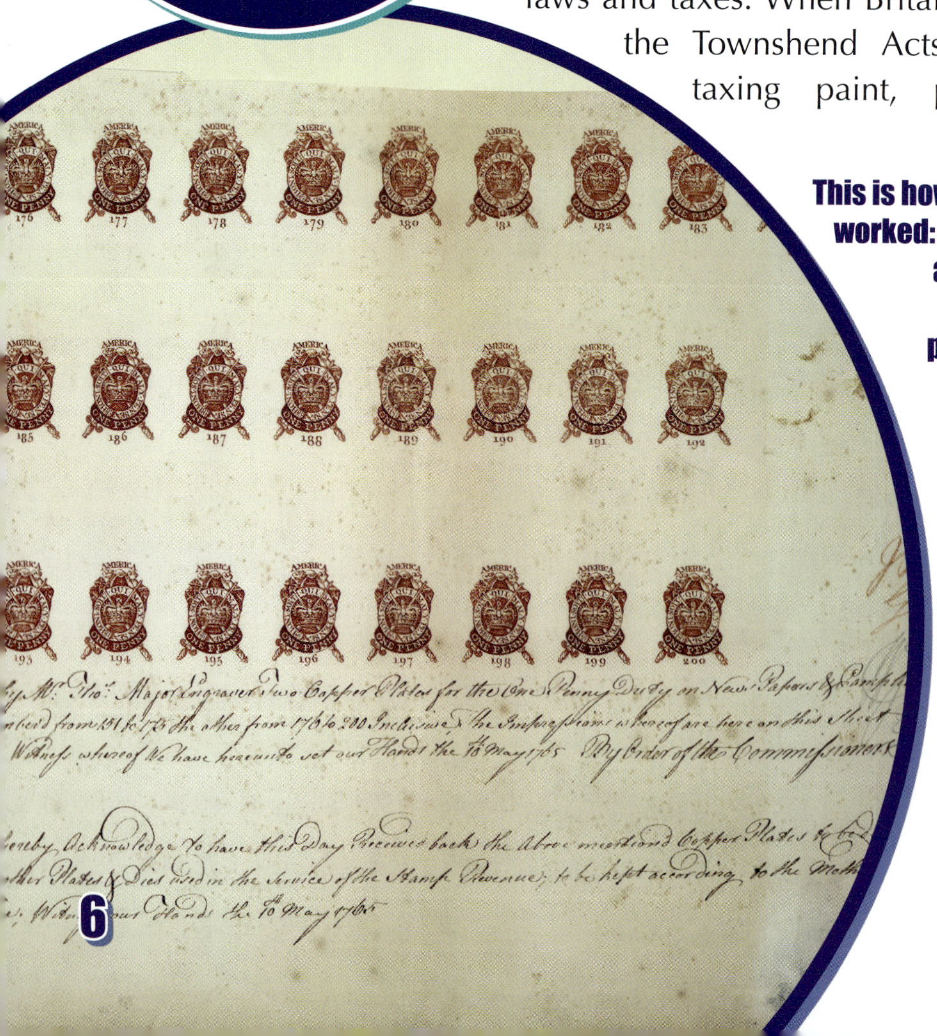

This is how the stamp tax worked: Stamps—such as those shown at left—were purchased from the British government and placed on documents, newspapers, and other items.

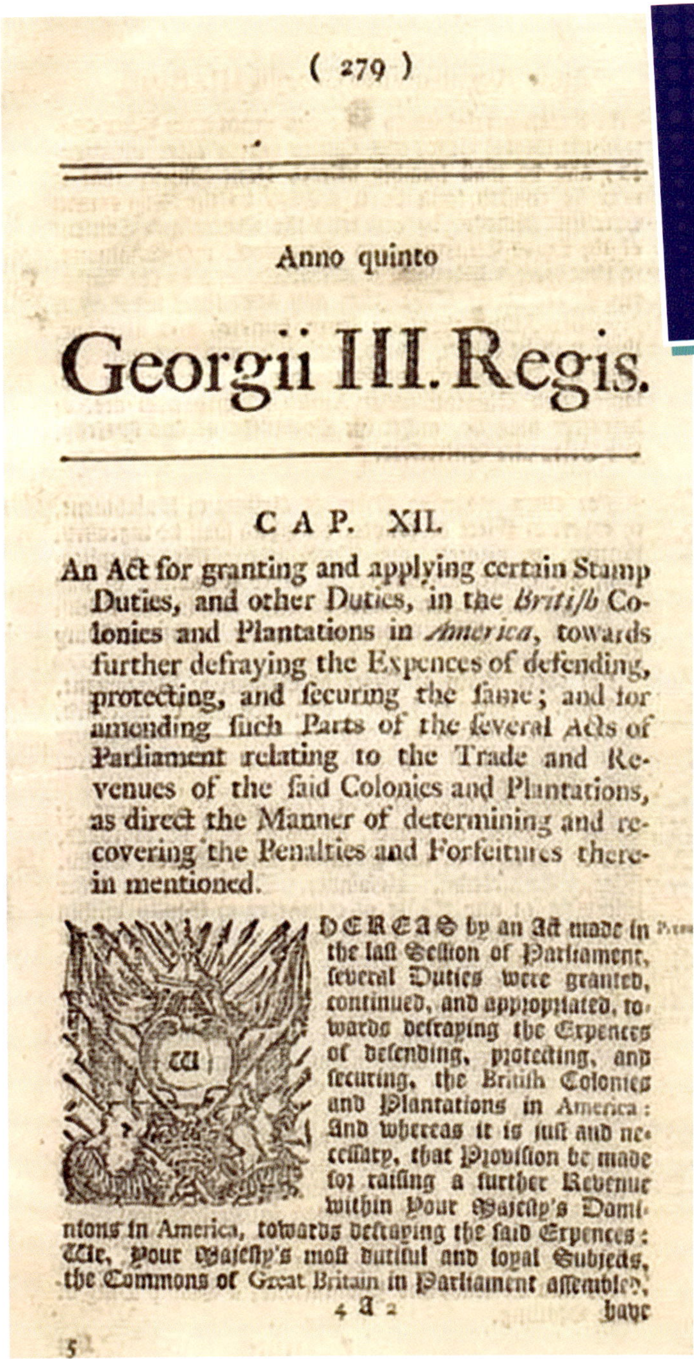
(279)

Anno quinto

Georgii III. Regis.

CAP. XII.

An Act for granting and applying certain Stamp Duties, and other Duties, in the *British* Colonies and Plantations in *America*, towards further defraying the Expences of defending, protecting, and securing the same; and for amending such Parts of the several Acts of Parliament relating to the Trade and Revenues of the said Colonies and Plantations, as direct the Manner of determining and recovering the Penalties and Forfeitures therein mentioned.

WHEREAS by an Act made in the last Session of Parliament, several Duties were granted, continued, and appropriated, towards defraying the Expences of defending, protecting, and securing, the British Colonies and Plantations in America: And whereas it is just and necessary, that Provision be made for raising a further Revenue within Your Majesty's Dominions in America, towards defraying the said Expences: We, Your Majesty's most dutiful and loyal Subjects, the Commons of Great Britain in Parliament assembled, have

4 A 2

Fast Fact

The Stamp Act inspired the Stamp Act Congress, which formed to ask Parliament and the British king to end the tax. It was the first such meeting of the colonies.

glass, and tea—the colonists began to act. Many boycotted certain British products, or refused to buy them in protest.

Erupting in Anger

Colonists labeling themselves "patriots" were ready to fight these British laws. The anger toward the Stamp Act was so great the British decided to abolish it in 1766. At the same time, Parliament asserted it had legislative, or lawmaking, power over the colonies.

The Stamp Act and the reasoning behind it was printed in colonial newspapers.

On March 5, 1770, a riot broke out when colonists began to throw sticks, snowballs, and stones at a British soldier. Additional British soldiers were called in to help, and they were attacked too. The soldiers then fired into the mob, killing five people. This incident became known as the Boston **Massacre**.

John Adams, the future president of the United States, was the lawyer for the British soldiers accused of murder. They were found not guilty of murder, though two were charged with **manslaughter**.

This 1770 engraving by Paul Revere depicts the event called the Boston Massacre. The British soldiers are shown firing on innocent Bostonians on purpose, though the court case revealed this is not what happened.

THE TEA PARTY

Patriots were eager to rebel against British control. Fighting broke out when Britain announced a complete **monopoly** on tea in the colonies. On December 16, 1773, patriots called the Sons of Liberty dressed as Native Americans and boarded ships in Boston Harbor. They dumped 342 cases of British tea into the water. The British punished the colonists by passing more laws in 1774. The **Coercive** Acts ordered the harbor closed until the colonists paid for the damage caused by this "Boston Tea Party." Because the colonists felt the Coercive Acts ignored their rights as British citizens, they renamed the laws the **Intolerable** Acts.

The Boston Tea Party destroyed an amount of tea that would be worth about $1.7 million today.

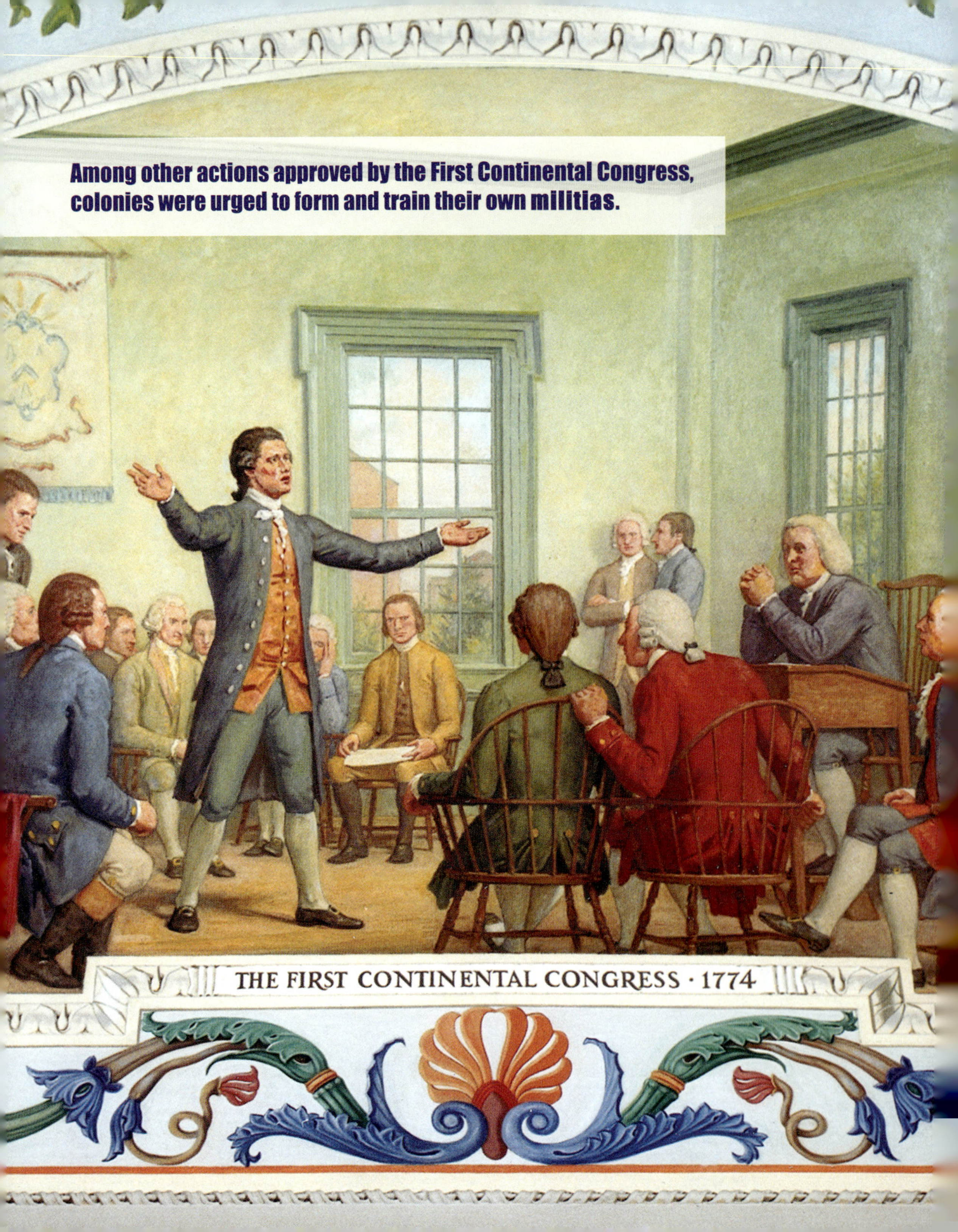

Among other actions approved by the First Continental Congress, colonies were urged to form and train their own militias.

THE WAR BEGINS

Chapter Two

Though the Coercive Acts were aimed at punishing Massachusetts colonists and stomping out rebellion there, they caused other colonies to side with Massachusetts. Leaders in the colonies decided to meet again. This time, the gathering was called the Continental Congress.

The First Continental Congress

On September 5, 1774, a group of colonial representatives gathered in Philadelphia, Pennsylvania. Each colony except Georgia sent delegates to this first Continental Congress. The Congress rejected taxation of the colonies without representation in Parliament and the presence of the British army without colonial agreement. The representatives approved of a boycott of all British products in the colonies and decided to stop exporting most colonial goods to Great Britain the following year. They also asked the British king, George III, for help.

George III was the king of Great Britain from 1760 to 1820.

Lexington and Concord

The patriots were ready to fight without disguises and out in the open. They collected weapons and other supplies. Some of these were stored in the town of Concord, Massachusetts. British soldiers—also called redcoats for their uniform color—received orders to take away or destroy these weapons.

> **Fast Fact**
>
> Some American militia were chosen to be "minutemen." This fighting force was supposed to be ready for battle at a "minute's notice."

By the time British troops reached the town of Lexington on April 19, 1775, they faced dozens of patriots from the Massachusetts militia, ready to fight. Shooting broke out, and eight Americans were killed. The British troops marched on to Concord, where they searched for weapons and **ammunition**. They destroyed what they found, though the colonists had hidden some.

No one knows who fired the first shots of the American Revolution.

A FAMOUS RIDE

On the night of April 18, 1775, Paul Revere—a patriot and messenger—set out to warn the people of Lexington and Concord of the redcoats' approach. He was to warn Samuel Adams and John Hancock of British orders for their arrest. He also arranged a signal: If the British came from Boston by land, one light would shine from the church tower of North Church. Two lights would appear if they approached by crossing the Charles River. That night, two lights were seen. Revere spread the news on horseback. Others did too. William Dawes and Revere were captured, but Samuel Prescott escaped to Concord.

Paul Revere was a Boston silversmith. He took part in the Boston Tea Party and was one of the Sons of Liberty.

When the British began their march back to Boston, they were met by more militia, about 400 fighters this time. Even farmers joined in the fight. In the end, about 274 British soldiers and 88 Americans were killed. The bloodshed caused many more colonists to become patriots. The American Revolution had begun.

Fast Fact

After the Battles of Lexington and Concord, about 20,000 militia soldiers from all over New England began to travel toward Boston to fight. They would become part of the Continental Army.

The Continental Congress and Army

On May 10, 1775, about a month after the first shots were fired at Lexington, the Second Continental Congress met in Philadelphia. This time, all 13 colonies sent representatives to discuss what actions to take next.

This Congress, including Samuel Adams, John Adams, John Hancock, Patrick Henry, Benjamin Franklin, and Thomas Jefferson, turned the New England militia into the main force of the colonial army, called the Continental Army. They made George Washington commander in chief of this army in June 1775. The Congress also issued new paper money. They borrowed money from countries overseas to pay soldiers and buy military supplies. This Congress acted as the first government of the united colonies.

Fast Fact

The Second Continental Congress sent a list of complaints and requests to King George III called the Olive Branch Petition. He refused to read it.

George Washington was respected for his leadership in the French and Indian War. The Congress also hoped Washington, a Virginian, could boost support for the war in the South.

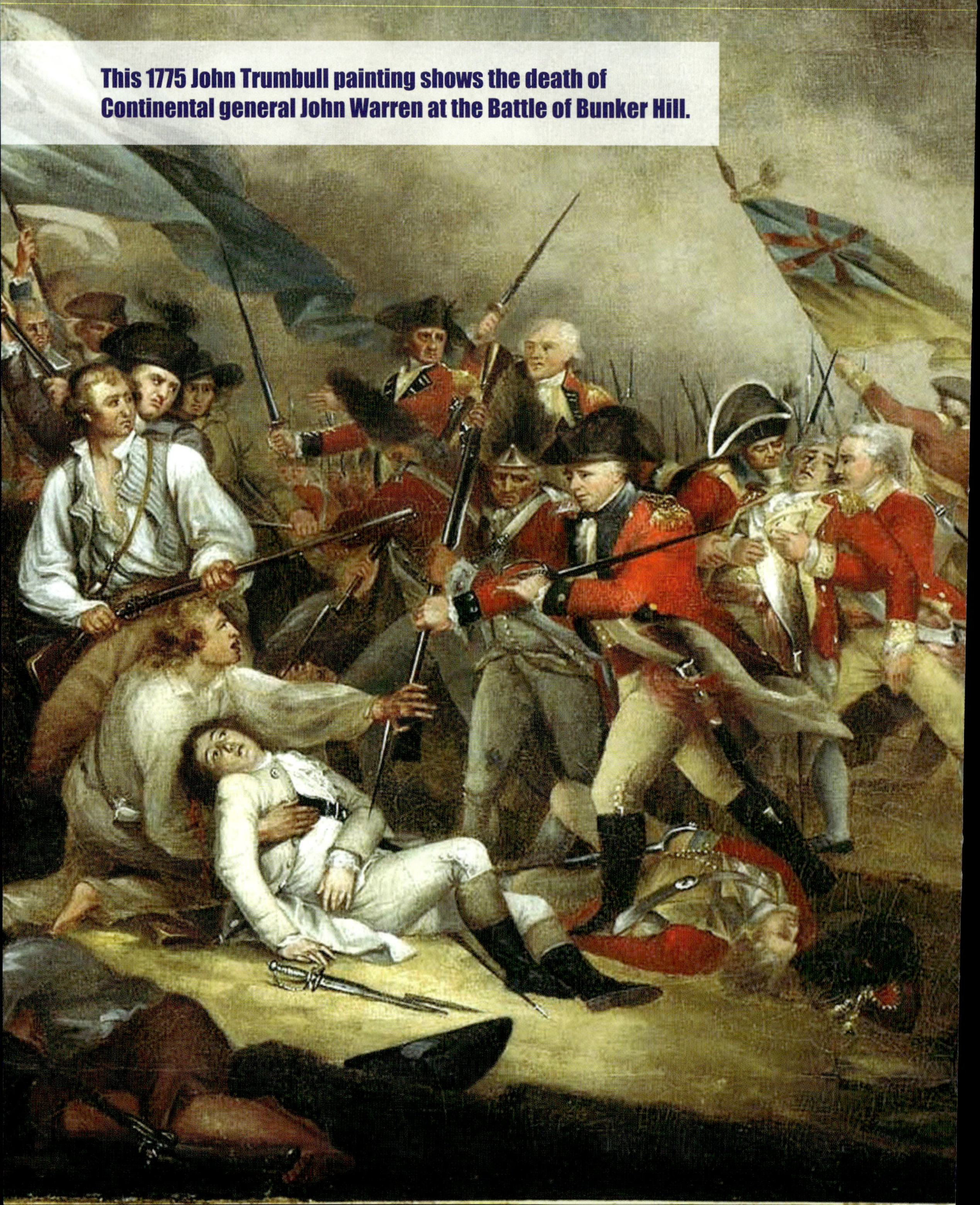

This 1775 John Trumbull painting shows the death of Continental general John Warren at the Battle of Bunker Hill.

THE REVOLUTION RAGES ON

Chapter Three

The Battle of Bunker Hill, sometimes called the Battle of Breed's Hill, was the first major battle of the American Revolution. An inexperienced Continental Army met British forces at Breed's Hill, across from Boston, in June 1775. This was an important site for control of the city.

First Tests of a New Army

By the evening of June 16, 1775, the Continental forces had taken position on Breed's Hill. The next day, they were fired on by British ships and then by redcoats on foot. The Americans held their ground. In the end, they ran out of ammunition and resorted to firing nails and glass at the British. (The battle was the origin of the famous phrase, "Don't fire until you see the whites of their eyes.") Even though the Americans retreated, they surprised the enemy, who had not expected much of a

Fast Fact

In November 1775, the Earl of Dunmore, governor of Virginia, promised freedom to any enslaved person who fought with the British army. Perhaps as many as 800 enslaved people escaped and enlisted.

Despite the fact that the battle took place mainly on and around Breed's Hill, it is known as the Battle of Bunker Hill. Bunker Hill was next to Breed's Hill. This 19th century painting shows the British trying to advance up the hill.

fight. The British won the battle, but lost hundreds more soldiers than the colonists.

In March 1776, a victory for Washington's army at Dorchester Heights forced the British from Boston into Canada. They would return.

A BESTSELLER

Thomas Paine moved from England to Pennsylvania in 1774. In January 1776, he published a **pamphlet** called *Common Sense*. In it, Paine challenged the idea of a king who held power over people. He argued that people should rule themselves. This principle of **democracy** became a cornerstone of the United States. More than 500,000 copies of *Common Sense* were sold. It swayed many colonists to support total independence from Great Britain. Paine also wrote a series of articles called the *American Crisis*. George Washington had the first powerful article read to his troops at Valley Forge. It started, "These are the times that try men's souls."

Fast Fact

John Hancock, president of the Second Continental Congress in 1776, was the first person to sign the Declaration of Independence.

The Declaration of Independence

By mid-1776, a peaceful solution to the conflict seemed impossible to many. By June, five representatives of the Second Continental Congress were assigned the task of writing a document outlining reasons why the colonies were asserting their independence from Great Britain. The Committee of Five included Benjamin Franklin, John Adams, Roger Sherman, Robert Livingston, and Thomas Jefferson.

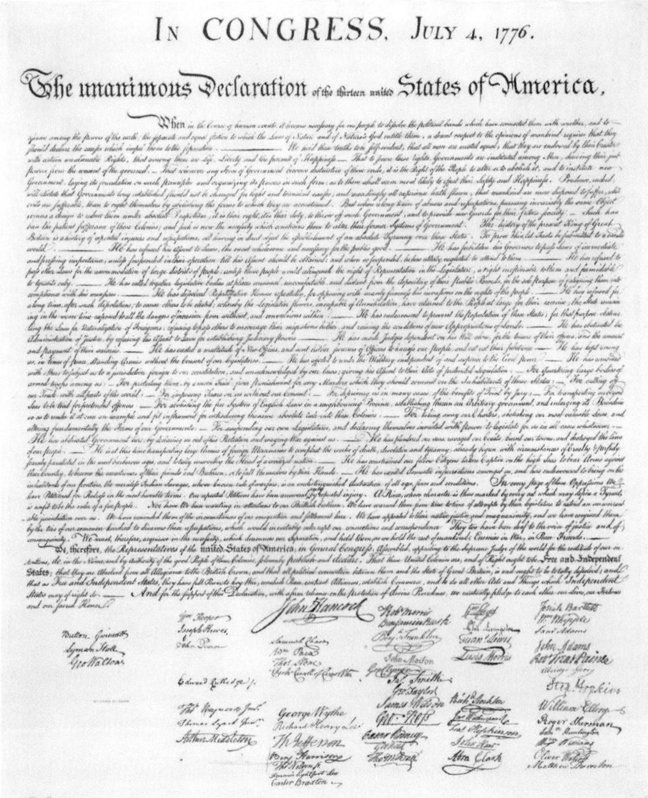
IN CONGRESS, JULY 4, 1776.

The unanimous Declaration of the thirteen united States of America,

The Declaration of Independence was later signed by 56 representatives of the "United States of America."

Mostly written by Thomas Jefferson, the Declaration of Independence said an unjust government must be "thrown off" if certain rights were threatened. Among those rights were "life, liberty, and the pursuit of happiness." Independence Day, or the Fourth of July, celebrates the day the Congress approved the wording of the Declaration of Independence.

Crossing the Delaware

Washington's rival at Dorchester Heights—General William Howe—landed in New York in July 1776 with 32,000 troops. At the Battle of Long Island, about 20,000 of these soldiers forced Washington's army into New York City. His troops were then driven into New Jersey. Pushed again—this time into Pennsylvania—the Continental Army's spirits were low. However, Washington had a plan.

Emanuel Leutze's *Washington Crossing the Delaware* (1851) is perhaps the most famous painting of the American Revolution.

Fast Fact

Women were nurses, spies, cooks, and even (disguised) soldiers in the American Revolution.

On the night of December 25, 1776, the colonial forces crossed the Delaware River into New Jersey. Washington knew that British allies, German soldiers called Hessians, were camped near Trenton. The Americans surprised and captured more than 900 enemy soldiers, not losing a single American life. Washington's forces moved farther into New Jersey, capturing Princeton. These victories boosted American spirits.

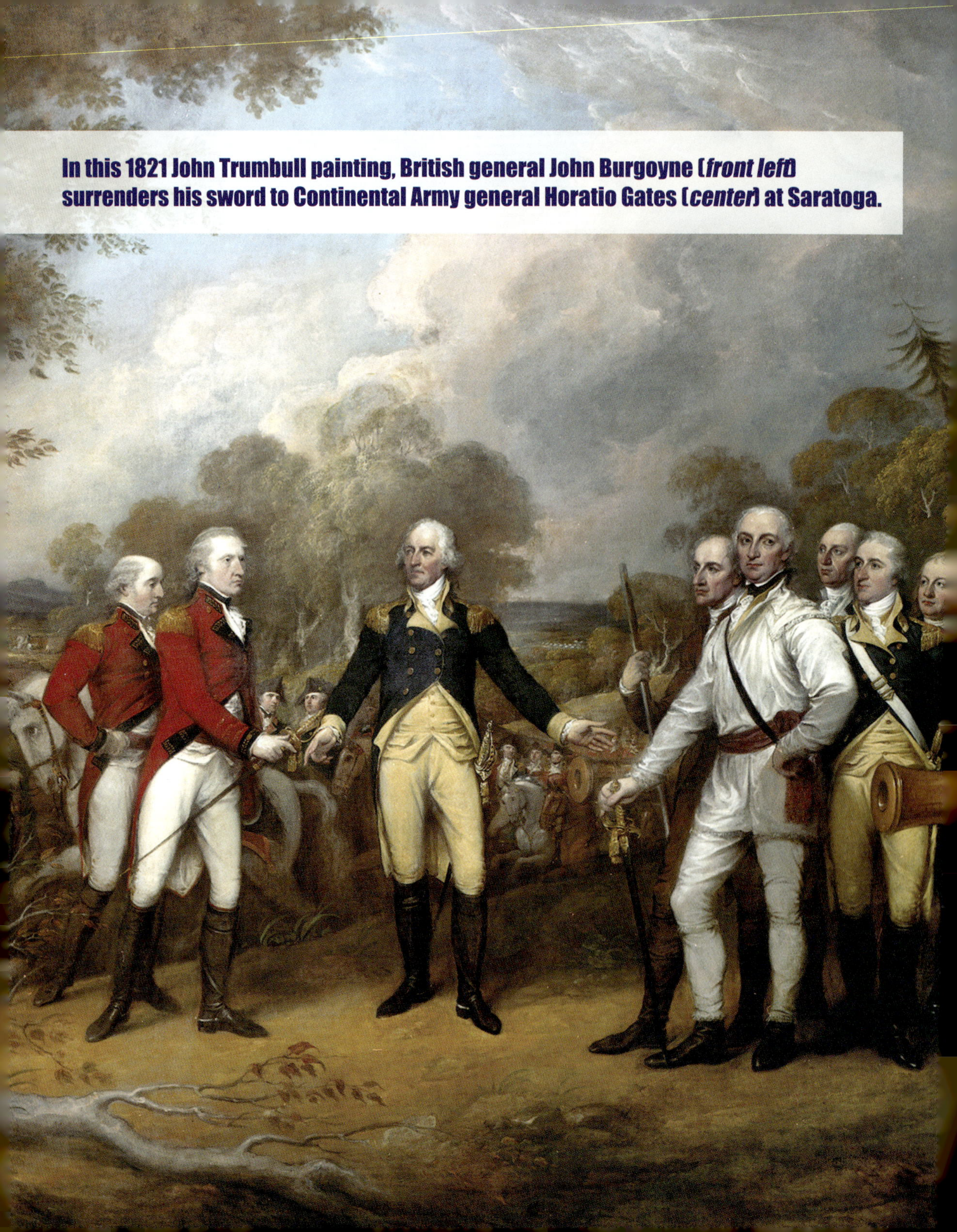

In this 1821 John Trumbull painting, British general John Burgoyne (*front left*) surrenders his sword to Continental Army general Horatio Gates (*center*) at Saratoga.

THE ROAD TO VICTORY

Chapter Four

In fall 1777, two battles in Pennsylvania—at Brandywine Creek and Germantown—ended in American defeats. Victory seemed far from certain for the colonists at this point. However, American forces stopped British general John Burgoyne's forces from marching across New York at the Battle of Saratoga. Burgoyne surrendered about 6,000 soldiers on October 17, 1777. The battle is considered to be the turning point of the revolution. It convinced France that the United States could win. France then promised to send aid and soldiers.

Valley Forge

The Continental Army under George Washington camped at Valley Forge in Pennsylvania during the winter of 1777–1778. Illness, lack of food and clothes, and freezing weather caused thousands to desert the army. Many died as well. Even horses starved to death. It was a dark time for the colonial forces.

Fast Fact

Benedict Arnold was a Continental Army general who helped the Americans win at Saratoga. He later switched sides and became a spy for the British.

Valley Forge is now a national historical park.

The winter had a positive side, though. While in France asking for aid, Benjamin Franklin met a German soldier named Frederick William Steuben. Franklin recommended Steuben to Washington as an experienced military leader. Steuben traveled to Valley Forge to train the Continental Army. By the summer of 1778, Washington's army was a better fighting force.

On June 28, 1778, the Continental Army fought its last major battle in the north at the Battle of Monmouth in New Jersey. There was no clear victor. However, the British began to focus their war efforts in the South where many loyalists—people who remained loyal to Britain—

Fast Fact

The Battle of Monmouth is remembered for the legend of Molly Pitcher. This was the nickname of a woman who carried pitchers of water to cool the battlefield cannons.

Some stories say Molly Pitcher took her husband's place at a cannon during battle.

lived. In December 1778, the Americans lost Savannah, Georgia. In 1780, the redcoats took the cities of Charleston and Camden in South Carolina too.

American general Nathanael Greene was given command of the southern Continental Army. He split up the Continental forces to battle against the British army under General Charles Cornwallis. Americans were the victors in the battles of Kings Mountain (October 1780) and Cowpens (January 1781) in South Carolina. The Battle of Guilford Courthouse in North Carolina in March 1781 was a British victory,

General Nathanael Greene's forces at the Battle of Guilford Courthouse included militias from North Carolina and Virginia as well as Continental Army "regulars."

but Cornwallis lost so many soldiers that he was forced to retreat into Virginia.

Decisive Victory

By mid-1781, Cornwallis had taken his British forces to the Yorktown peninsula in Virginia. The Continental Army and French forces were presented with an opportunity. Thousands of soldiers moved to surround Yorktown. The French navy created a **blockade** on the water.

Cornwallis surrendered on October 19, 1781, ending the last major battle of the war. Some fighting still took place. However, the war had become unpopular in Britain, and Parliament finally agreed to end the conflict. By 1783, the American Revolution was over.

PEACE OF PARIS

Following the fighting, the terms of the treaty between the nations had to be decided. Benjamin Franklin, John Adams, and John Jay traveled to Paris, France, to meet with British officials. On September 3, 1783, the American Revolution officially ended with the signing of a treaty between Great Britain and the United States. Great Britain formally recognized the United States as an independent country. The treaty also named the Mississippi River as the new nation's western boundary. The United States of America was free. Now the task before the Americans was to create a nation that honored the ideals for which they had fought.

Fast Fact

Marie Joseph Paul Yves Roch Gilbert du Motier—the Marquis de Lafayette—sailed to the American colonies in 1777 to help the Continental Army. He played a major part in persuading the French to give aid to the Americans.

British general Charles Cornwallis was not at the surrender ceremony. He sent his second in command, Brigadier General Charles O'Hara (*middle center, in red*). General Benjamin Lincoln (*middle, on horseback*) accepted the surrender for the American forces.

A TIMELINE OF THE AMERICAN REVOLUTION

1763 The French and Indian War ends.

1764 The Sugar Act is passed.

1765 The Stamp Act is passed.

1770 The Boston Massacre occurs.

1773 The Boston Tea Party occurs.

1774 The First Continental Congress meets following the Coercive Acts.

1775 The Battles of Lexington and Concord begin the war on April 19.

1775 The Second Continental Congress meets beginning May 10.

1775 The Battle of Bunker Hill ends in a hard-fought British victory in June.

1776 The Declaration of Independence is approved on July 4.

1776 In December, George Washington crosses the Delaware River with troops to secure a victory in Trenton.

1777 An American victory is declared at Saratoga in October.

1777–1778 The Continental Army spends a difficult winter in Valley Forge.

1778 In June, the Battle of Monmouth has no clear victor.

1781 The British surrender at Yorktown.

1783 The Treaty of Paris is signed.

THINK ABOUT IT!

1. Do you think the colonies should have shared in the cost of British wars? Why or why not?
2. Do you think the American Revolution would have occurred if the colonies had been granted representation in Parliament? Explain your reasoning.
3. As many as one-fifth of Americans were loyalists, supporting the British. Why do you think they remained loyal while others wanted freedom?
4. How might the involvement of other countries have affected the outcome of the war?

GLOSSARY

ammunition: Bullets, shells, and other objects used as weapons.

blockade: The blocking of harbors to keep people and supplies from coming and going.

coercive: Using force to make people do things against their will.

commence: To begin.

democracy: The free and equal right of every person to participate in a government.

intolerable: So bad, difficult, or painful that it cannot be endured.

manslaughter: The illegal killing of another person without advance planning.

massacre: The cruel killing of a large number of people.

militia: A military force composed of citizens, used in emergencies.

monopoly: A situation in which only one company controls an industry or product.

pamphlet: A small book that gives information.

Parliament: The lawmaking body of Great Britain.

FIND OUT MORE

Books

Gagne, Tammy. *Fact and Fiction of the American Revolution.* Minneapolis, MN: Abdo Publishing, 2022.

Marsh, Sarah Glenn. *Anna Strong: A Spy During the American Revolution.* New York, NY: Abrams Books for Young Readers, 2020.

Murray, Stuart. *American Revolution.* New York, NY: DK Publishing, 2022.

Websites

The Road to Revolution
www.pbs.org/ktca/liberty/road.html
Test your knowledge of the time period on this PBS site.

The Roles of Women in the Revolutionary War
historyofmassachusetts.org/the-roles-of-women-in-the-revolutionary-war/
Read about the essential parts that women played during this time.

Timeline of the Revolution
www.nps.gov/subjects/americanrevolution/timeline.htm
Read about more crucial events that led to the American victory.

INDEX